Every Planet Has a Place

A Book About Our Solar System

BY

BECKY BAINES

NATIONAL GEOGRAPHIC

Washington, D.C.

Every planet has a place in space.

Jupiter

Ceres

Earth

Mercury

Venus

Mars

Uranus

Pluto

Saturn

Neptune

Eris

A planet is a round object that circles a star.

The planets race, one by one, in their rings around the Sun.

Everything in our solar system is in orbit around the Sun.

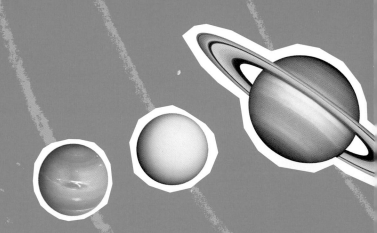

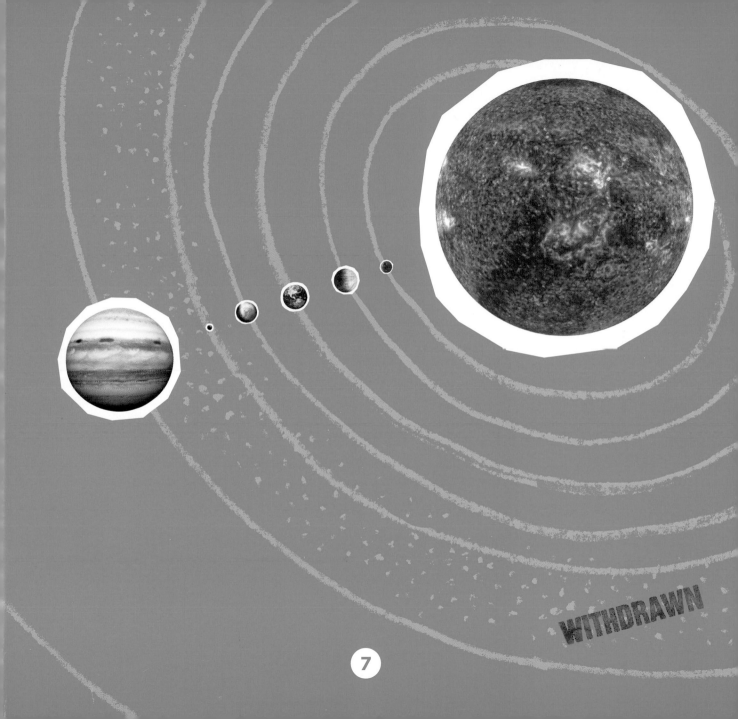

7

The Sun's a star so hot and bright it sends us lots of heat and light.

The Sun, and everything in our solar system (even us!), is made of the exploded leftovers of ancient stars. We are made of old stardust!

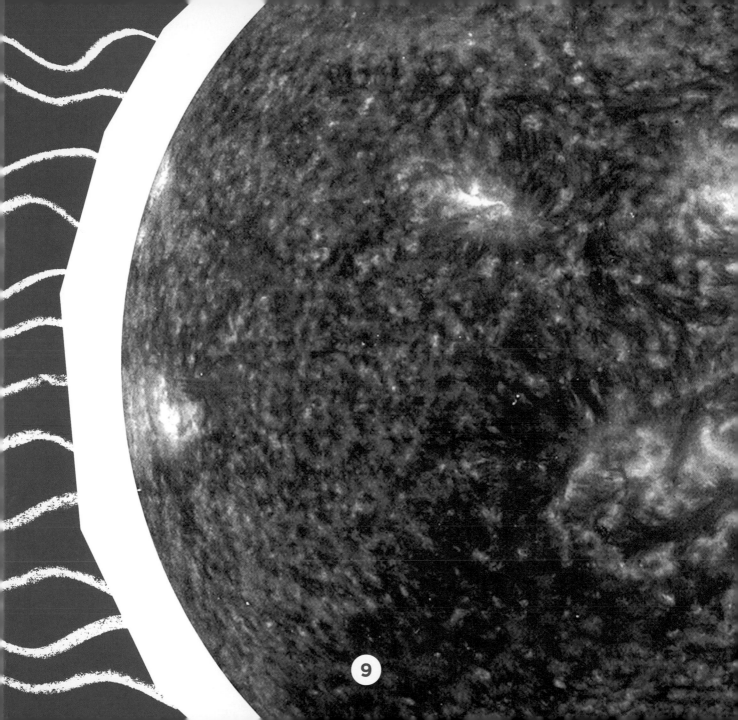

Nearest the Sun

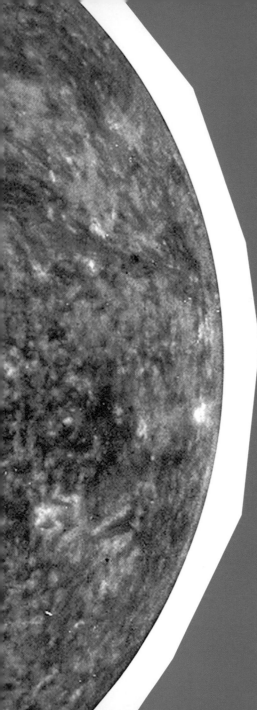

1.

Mercury

Venus is covered with volcanoes.

2.

Venus

If you weigh 70 pounds on Earth, you would weigh 27 pounds on Mercury.

are four planet worlds made mostly out of rock.

Earth

3.

Home, sweet home

Mars is red because it's made of iron and it's rusty. It even has a rusty pink sky!

4.

Mars

JUST
RIGHT!

The third—our Earth —has just the right spot—not too cold, not too hot.

The heat and light Earth gets from the Sun make it just right for life.

The asteroid belt is mostly rocks circling the Sun.

And how many dwarf planets does it have? Count! You'll find just one.

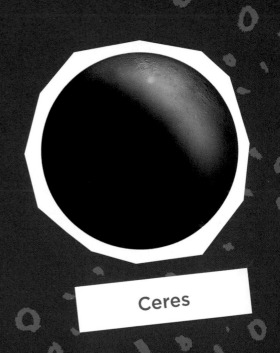

Ceres

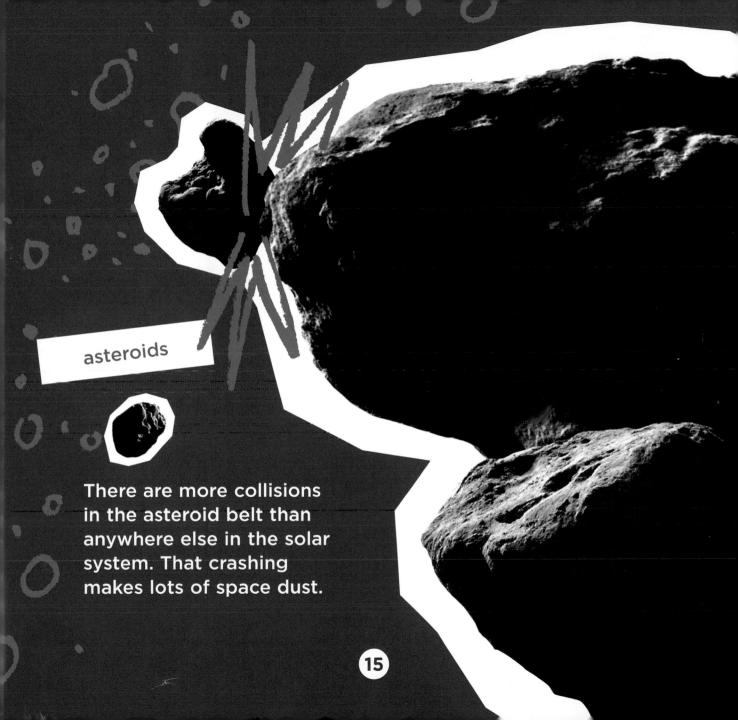

asteroids

There are more collisions
in the asteroid belt than
anywhere else in the solar
system. That crashing
makes lots of space dust.

15

Jupiter is the biggest planet in the solar system. 1,300 Earths could fit inside it.

Jupiter

Out beyond the asteroids, four gas giants whirl.

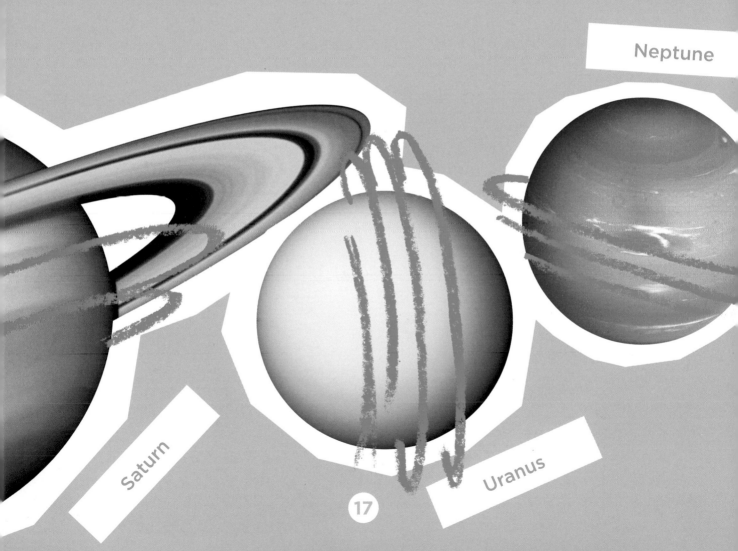

Neptune

Saturn

Uranus

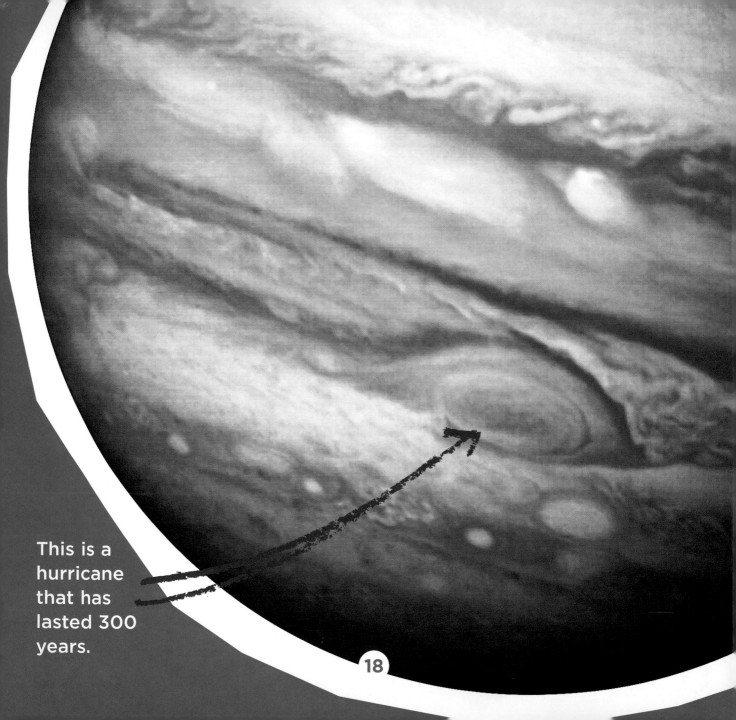

This is a hurricane that has lasted 300 years.

They have wild, wild weather...

The gas giants are not solid —they are clouds of gas. The clouds on Jupiter move faster than hurricane winds on Earth.

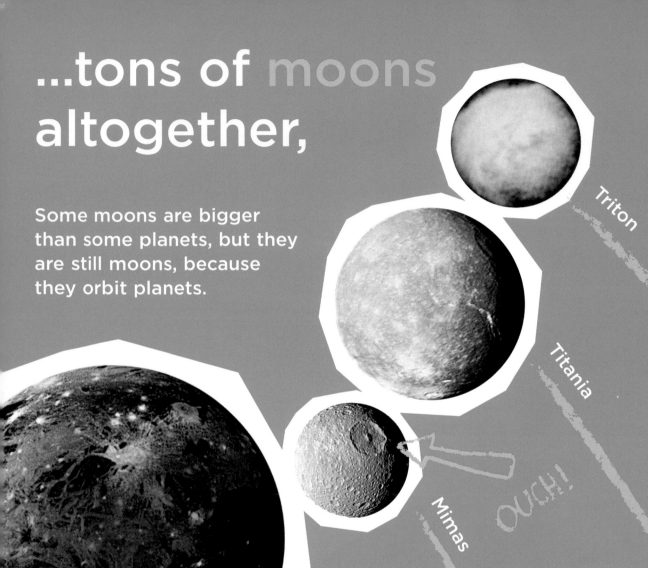

...tons of moons altogether,

Some moons are bigger than some planets, but they are still moons, because they orbit planets.

Triton

Titania

Mimas

OUCH!

Ganymede

and enormous rings that swirl.

All the gas giants have rings. Saturn's rings are made of bits of dust-covered ice. Some pieces are as small as dust, some are bigger than houses!

21

What comes next?
The Kuiper belt,
full of comets
and rocks,
and two dwarf
planets hiding
like toys in a
cereal box.

Some comets,
like Halley's,
come from here.

THIS WAY
TO THE SUN

10 BILLION MILES

Eris

Pluto

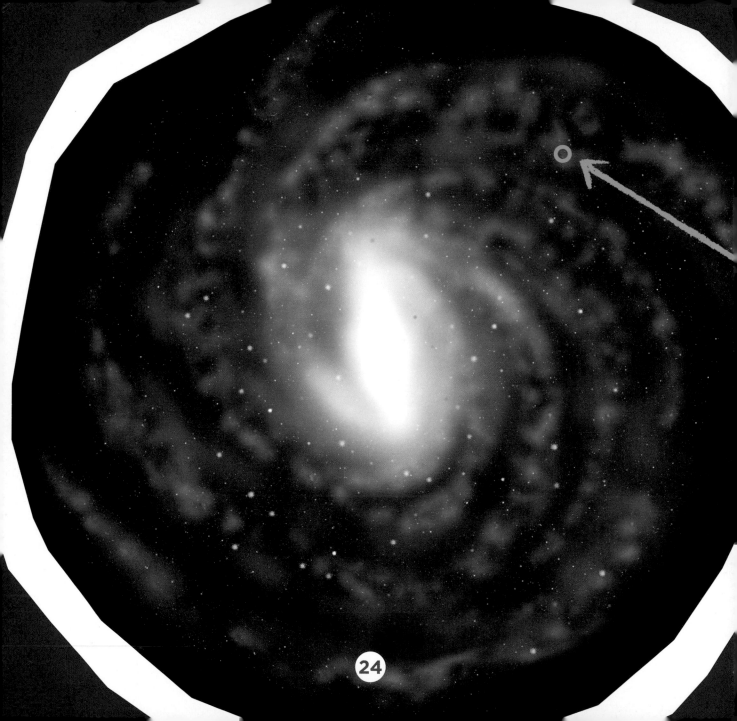

24

Now look at this picture and see us in the Milky Way Galaxy.

Our whole solar system sits here, in a cloud called the Local Fluff.

Our Sun is just one of 400 billion stars in the galaxy, and the Milky Way Galaxy is one of billions of galaxies in outer space.

It's nice to know, in our corner of space, that every planet has a place.

27

Zigzag through these ideas for more thoughts about our solar system.

What do you think it would feel like to float in space?

If you could live on another planet, which one would you choose?

If your bed is the Sun, what's Earth?

Draw a spaceship that would keep you safe through the asteroid belt.

What do you think the Earth would look like if you were standing on Venus?

What do you think space sounds like?

Pretend you are the Sun! Swing a yo-yo above your head in a circle. The yo-yo is like a planet.

Star light, star bright, first star I see at night. Wish I may, wish I might, have the wish I wish tonight.

Look at the moon a few nights in a row. Watch how it changes. Is it growing or shrinking?

What would happen if we had no sun?

National Geographic's net proceeds support vital exploration, conservation, research, and education programs.

Published by The National Geographic Society
1145 17th Street, N.W.
Washington, D.C. 20036
Visit us online at www.nationalgeographic.com/books

Design: fuszion

Printed in the United States of America

Library of Congress Cataloging-in-Publication Data

Baines, Rebecca.
  Every Planet Has a Place : A Book About Our Solar System / by Becky Baines.
    p. cm. — (A Zig Zag Book)
  ISBN 978-1-4263-0313-5 (hardcover : alk. paper) —
ISBN 978-1-4263-0314-2 (lib. bdg. : alk. paper)
1. Solar system—Juvenile literature. I. Title.
QB501.3.B347 2008
523.2—dc22
2008024447

Photo Credits
All artwork by David A. Aguilar
unless otherwise noted below:

Corbis/ NASA: 6 center, 6 far right, 11 left, 12, 16-17, 17 center, 18-19, 20 right
Getty Images/ NASA: 4 far left, 4 left, 6 right, 7 right center, 7 right, 10 center, 10 right, 17 right, 20 far right
Getty Images/ Antonio M. Rosario: 21
iStockPhoto: 4 (3rd from left), 7 center, 24 (3rd from left)
NASA: 7 far right, 9, 10 far left, 20 far left, 20 left, 23 right
Shutterstock: 7 far left, 16 left

To Amy and Nancy— two editors who are out of this world.
—B.B.